THE POWER OF POSITIVE CHRISTIAN TEACHING

THE POWER OF POSITIVE CHRISTIAN TEACHING

DONALD P. MARSOLAIS

XULON ELITE

Xulon Press Elite
2301 Lucien Way #415
Maitland, FL 32751
407.339.4217
www.xulonpress.com

Exulon
ELITE

Printed in the United States of America.

ISBN-13: 978-1-66280-122-8

DEDICATION

This book is dedicated to Brandie Auernig and Sister Arlene Connolly, IBVM.

It was Brandie who, when she found out that I would be leaving Holy Family Catholic School, suggested this book as a way of passing on my techniques, strategies, and methods to other teachers and parents. Brandie, thank you for your words of encouragement and support. Without your suggestion, I doubt that I would have written this book. The fact that you believed in my methods made me ask myself who else might benefit from reading about my techniques and strategies for achieving both student and teacher success in the classroom. Thank you!

Sister Arlene Connolly, IBVM hired me to teach at Holy Family Catholic School. She believed that I could handle her 7th grade after only one year of teaching. I had known and worked with Sister for many years as our youngest son went through all of his elementary school years at Holy Family School. Sister, without your support and belief in my skill level, this book would not have been possible. Thank you!

TABLE OF CONTENTS

INTRODUCTION

THE DAY IS FRIDAY, JUNE 4, 2010. IT'S THE last day of school at Holy Family Catholic School in Citrus Heights, California, as well as my last day teaching 7th and 8th grade language arts and religion. I'm leaving the school not by choice, but rather by request.

No, I didn't swear at a student or create any problem for the principal. I just happened to be one of nine teachers who had been asked not to return due to a poor economy that had created very low enrollment. Our school used to be the largest in the Sacramento Diocese, but not any longer. We went from having two classes in each grade K-8 to, next year, one class per grades K-8. We went from close to 650 students down to approximately 280 students next year. Obviously, something had to change in order to be able to pay the bills. This was really a long time coming and overdue.

My nine years of seniority was no challenge to my partner 7th grade teacher with over 30 years experience. Needless to say, the last week of school was an emotional roller coaster. I love teaching and think that I am pretty good at it. I would continue if I could and, even as I begin writing this book, my resumes have been sent out to approximately 20 schools in the Diocese. The difficulty is that most Catholic schools are suffering from low enrollment. I expect that I may have taught my last class unless something extraordinary occurs.

While I do have nine years experience, becoming a teacher was my third career. Following a four year stint in the US Air Force during the Viet Nam War era, I enjoyed an eight year career working in management at United California Bank. I was able to move from the Bank to Pacific Telephone where I retired after 21 good years also in management. During the 29 years of my first two careers, I spent most of my time training others; teaching others.

I really always wanted to be a teacher, but, as it often does, life got in the way. By the time I left the Air Force I was married and had a responsibility to provide for my family. I needed a job. While working at the Bank, I used the GI Bill to pay for a Bachelor's Degree in English

(1975) and a Masters Degree in Public Administration (1980) from California State University Dominguez Hills. My goal was to teach English at the high school level, but my goal changed when I was offered an opportunity to work at the bank's headquarters.

I gained a lot of skill and learned a lot of techniques while training at the bank and the telephone company. I was sent to many schools and was instrumental in creating seminars and programs to enhance employee satisfaction with their jobs. I was a natural choice for these assignments because of my ability to speak in front of both small and large groups; a skill I learned at Toastmaster's while earning the Boy Scouts' highest honor, the Eagle Badge.

As I retired from Pacific Bell at the age of 52, my desire to teach was resurrected. After dabbling in several meaningless jobs, my wife finally convinced me to follow my heart and apply to the Diocese of Sacramento for a job as a teacher. While I didn't have a California Teaching Credential, I had a Masters Degree and was going to pursue the credential if I got hired. To my surprise, I was hired within three months of submitting my application.

As I taught during the next nine years, I learned many valuable lessons from teachers, parents, and students. I learned that teaching is an attitude surrounded by process and passion. The best teachers do all they can to understand each of their students as individuals - What makes them tick? What is going on at home? What extra help do they need?

This book is being written to compile the techniques, strategies, and methods I have used effectively over nineteen years teaching all types of learners. My goal when I began teaching was to make a difference. Based on feedback from many parents and students, I have accomplished my goal. It never ceases to amaze me who "got it" and is thankful for the effort I put in as their teacher.

In 2010, I met one of my former students who was graduating from high school. When she saw me, she ran over, gave me a big hug, and couldn't contain herself. She had just received a scholarship to the University of California Santa Cruz to study Literature. Her exact quote to me was, "*Tom Sawyer* in your 7th grade class changed my life. I never used to read, but after reading *Tom Sawyer* with you in class, I couldn't get enough. Thank you, Mr. Marsolais."

Many of the things in this book may not be new to you, but if even just one technique helps you to make a difference, this book will have been worth it. All I know is that my methods, strategies, and techniques have been applauded by administrators, parents, and students alike.

So, I'm back to June 4, 2010, the last day of school, and a student that I had two years on student council but never in the classroom, gave me a cake that she and her mother baked. I had taught her sister and brother in previous years. The card that came with the cake was the culmination of a week's worth of good wishes. Just another farewell card I thought, but the mom summed up my career at Holy Family by acknowledging my unique, caring style of teaching and suggested that I write a book and maybe go out on a speaking tour to share what I know. Her final comment in the card was, "You have made a difference in both students and families alike." Remember my goal – to make a difference? It was nice to be validated.

My heart was so touched with this family's faith in my abilities that I decided to spend the time I would have on unemployment to write the book they wanted. As I prepared my outline and created my notes, it became more obvious to me that this is a book that may inspire all teachers regardless of tenure. Each teacher has their own way of teaching, but it's my hope that these techniques will add to a teacher's body of knowledge on how to create a classroom of dedicated learners.

While typing out the first draft of this manuscript, I was offered a part-time position at several other Catholic schools and finally returned to the classroom as a 6th grade teacher at Saint Joseph Catholic School in Auburn, California. The first thing I did was put this book on the shelf as I decided to gather more information during my next assignment to add to the uncompleted manuscript.

It is now July 8, 2020, and I have picked up my draft again to finish it and publish it. I love teaching, but, at 73 with sporadic health problems, I chose to retire so as not to potentially impact the school. Retirement doesn't mean finished to me. It simply means a new challenge in life. Finishing this book seems to be it. I may even get the opportunity to speak on this book.

My guess is that parents will also find this book useful as many of these techniques can be used at home to help with behavior and/or achieving success in the classroom. A child's education is a partnership between student, parents, and teacher. All three working together can create the success that all desire.

My time spent teaching in the Diocese of Sacramento was extremely rewarding, mostly because I was able to practice my faith on a daily basis as I taught my students. I hope that my insights from the classroom help each of you add to your existing skills, expand your desire to teach our nation's next generation using these Christian methods, and make your own difference in their lives.

It all Starts with Respect

What's your perspective on respect? There are those who say that you have to earn it before you give it and you get it. Others say that all are worthy of respect and they treat everyone that way. What's the correct approach for a classroom of students?

I hear you all splitting the choices. Some of you are taking the path that leads to placing your whole class in a pot on the first day of school and maybe giving them the benefit of the doubt, but waiting to see if they deserve your respect. Then there are the rest of you who assume a respect for your students from day one and you treat them that way.

Before I started teaching, I was told by those who supposedly knew, not to get into Junior High because "those kids have no respect." If I was a person who believed in everything I was told, I would probably not have ever had the great experience of teaching Junior

High students. What I found was that students come into a new year of school truly looking to make a new start with whoever the teacher is.

They walk in, backpacks full of supplies, eager to please their new mentor. It doesn't take them long to reconnect with their friends from previous years and, together, decide what the new teacher is all about. On what do you think that they base their perception? I say perception because that is exactly all they have to go on – that and reputation.

What you do on day one can help to set the tone for the entire year. What do you do on day one? Is it a day full of you giving your new class your rules and expectations? Of course, you have to let students know those things, but how do you go about it? Is your approach one of "sit down, be quiet, listen, and take notes" or do you encourage students to interact with you and each other during the first hour or so? The difference between demanding total respect before you know your students at all and getting to know them a little first can help create a class where respect is given and gotten almost automatically.

Here's the process I used to get to know my students on the first day of school. First, there were no desks in place. Chairs were placed in a circle so that we were all part of the same "learning wheel." Music was playing in the background when they came in. Usually, it's the music that I liked and was used all year when students entered the classroom. Music sets a tone that you are open to new and different approaches.

Once it is time to start class, invite all to take a seat. Yes, I said invite. Why start off on the wrong foot by making a demand of your first interaction with them? It's all in how you approach it. You could say something as simple as, "Good morning class. Would you please take a seat so we can get started." The worst start would be something like, "Seats, please!" and then proceed to direct students to the chair you want them to sit in. Which approach do you think that students would respond to best in the long run? Remember, your first interaction should be all about how you respect them. You can't just say the words. Actions tell the tale.

So now you have them in a circle and you're ready to see who's in attendance. The easiest way is to simply call the roll and let each respond with the ever popular, "Here!" That gets the job done, but here is a twist that will help you to get to know your students and give them an opportunity to know that they are in a special class or at least a class that's different from others that they may have been in before.

Know in advance how many students you have in your class. Have the exact number of chairs in place before your students enter. When they take their seats you will know whether all are present or if someone is absent. Invite them to introduce themselves and tell you one thing that you may want to know about them. That may be anything from what subject they like best in school to what sports they play to what ice cream flavor they like best. Always, always, always start with your own introduction giving them the same information that you are asking for. Do not go overboard. Now is not the time to let them know all about yourself. That will come later in the morning.

As students introduce themselves, check off the attendance roster. You will find that by focusing on what your students are telling you, it will be easier to remember their names (at least their first names.) My goal on the first day was to know each of my students' names by the end of the day. That is a measure of respect that students pick up on. By making an attempt to know them by name, you are telling them that you care about respecting them.

The easiest way to ensure that you know all your students' names by the end of the first day is to simply go around the room calling off names at random intervals. It's a pretty simple way of breaking up the morning. You'll find that each time you go around the room you will know more and more. I found that I knew all my students (30 or so) by about the third time around the room. To make it more challenging for you and fun for your students, have them change places if they want, then go around the room seeing how much you remember.

Once again while still in the circle, respect that your students already know most of the school rules. Invite (there's that word again) them to share what the rules are. Select a different student for each rule. Make sure and use their name. It will help you achieve your goal of knowing them all by name by the end of the day. Get as many students involved as possible. When they are finished, highlight the most important rules, any that they may have forgotten, and any new rules that they need to know.

If you are teaching in a Catholic or other religious school, you need to spend a few moments talking about the respect that is expected for your faith and the people in leadership such as priests, pastors, nuns, sisters, deacons, etc. This should only take a few minutes. You can let students know how important this is to your school by sharing your own involvement in the Parish. By sharing this, you are letting your students know that respect is important for more than just each other, you, and other teachers.

If you have a special place to pray on campus or a chapel that is associated with your church, take your students on a "field trip." Who doesn't like a field trip on the first day of school? We had a prayer garden at Holy Family School that was the perfect place to take students on the first day to let them know that prayer and faith are an important part of their education. Most will appreciate the opportunity to come together in prayer as a class on the first day. You could have prayed in class, but this effort will be an outward sign of your respect for them.

After introductions, sharing, and praying together, it's probably time for recess. Just prior to recess I would surprise my students with donuts. Hold on, hold on. I can hear you now. "He's buying their respect with food." I suppose you could look at it that way, but there is another perspective worth exploring. Most every one of our family get-togethers include food, right? Food and love is an important "glue" that holds families together. What better way to show your kids on day one that you think of them as family than by sharing some food with them? Think about it.

The rest of the day is used to continue making students comfortable with the Junior High environment and what they can expect throughout the rest of the school year.

On day two, place the desks in whatever arrangement you feel is most conducive to group education. Some teachers place desks in rows. Others place them in pods of four or six. Still others place desks on either side of the classroom facing each other with the center of the room open. It doesn't matter how you originally arrange your desks so long as you are open to making one or two changes throughout the school year that include input from your students. By allowing them to input into the new classroom organization, you are telling students that you respect their decisions and you expect their buy-in to make it work.

In conclusion, as you give respect, so shall it be returned to you. Respect your students as people first and students second from day one and see what a great year you have.

Respect Challenge:

Take an opportunity to bring your class together in a circle to discuss things that are going on in the class. You can call this a class meeting or simply just a way of touching bases. Make it something different from the normal way you share and ask your students to share. You can do this either inside or outside. Let them know that you respect their opinions. Gather the information you need from them and act on what you can and ask them to act on what they can. This type of check-in lets your students know that you value their input as family members.

Not Me and Them, But Us

So now what? You've built a framework of respect in the class that is meant to be a two-way street. How do your students know what the year will be like? It's simple. You lay it out for them.

You let them know that you are there for them no matter what their needs. It seems like a no-brainer, but too often we tend to merely answer questions regarding the lessons and ignore other things that may be going on in the classroom.

Students rely on us more than we know. They rely on us to be a safe haven for their concerns no matter how great or how small. Teaching can't just be about what's in the books. Teaching has to be about life lessons just as much as about "book learnin'." How do we do that without it being a curriculum subject? How can we help them through issues that are bothering them if we don't know what they are?

It's pretty simple if you think about it. Just look and listen to what's going on in the classroom. It's amazing what you'll see and hear that can help you short-circuit problems before they blow out of control. Wouldn't you like to know if Janie and Margie are having some personal problems that need to be attended to long before one of them does or says something that they may regret later?

While some students may not want to confide in you on their own, most will when asked the simple questions, "What's going on? You look a little upset." They may say "nothing" or they may open up. In either case, you need to be prepared to follow-up until you are satisfied that you have been able to help or that there truly is "nothing" going on.

Students will feel more comfortable answering your questions if you have established an "us" attitude in the classroom. We, all students and classroom teacher, are in this together. So, let's make things better together.

By establishing with your students that "we" are in this together at the beginning of the year, the concept of "us" can be an easy concept to explain. This also needs to be explained to parents at the open-house meeting. As you all know, parents are the primary educators of their children and we work in partnership with both the parents and students to achieve learning success.

Many teachers see their role in the classroom as the teacher and that's all. In truth, we are teachers, but, to our students, we are so much more than that. We have them in class almost as much as their parents have them awake at home. That gives us a special responsibility to "parent" them as well as teach them. We do this by being interested in their needs and offering assistance when we can. We can't do that if we are not in tune with what's going on in the classroom.

There is a valuable byproduct to being interested in what is going on in the classroom. That's trust. By letting your students know that you care about them and their problems, you will build trust that will enhance the respect that you are giving them.

It's easy to say, "I trust you," but how do you demonstrate that trust? For teachers, it's saying what you mean, and meaning what you say. By following this simple rule, you will eliminate confusion in your students' minds. Never say anything that you don't mean. Choosing to handle a classroom disruption by working on building trust can make a world of difference in both your student and class life.

"You'd better stop talking, or I'm sending you to the principal," or "giving you detention," or "taking away your recess," or any other negative enforcers you can think of need to be applied. The students keep talking and never go to the office or get what "punishment" you offered them. What are they to think? At first, they believe that you may apply it, but after seeing you in action, or non-action, you have given them permission to continue with the behavior.

Now look at the other side of the coin. You actually do punish the students for talking in class. You have done what you said you would do, but what have you gained? Sure, you have made an example of them, but what is the class thinking of your "us" concept? Everything you do in class has to be based on mutual respect and trust. Sometimes you give it more than you get it, but you must never break from the goal of creating an "us" environment.

What other way can you think of to handle a student who disrupts the class by talking? Think of a way that also builds respect and trust.

Before continuing this chapter, stop here. Write down a few ways you may have of handling this particular problem. Remember that what you are attempting to do is solve the behavior problem while building respect and trust in the student. Whatever you think of doing, remember to "say what you mean, and mean what you say."

Thanks for doing the exercise. I bet that you found at least two different ways to handle this problem without using negative reinforcement. Let me tell you what I have learned about fixing this particular problem.

Remembering that I am looking to build respect and trust in my students, I would ask them to step outside. Because of what it usually means when asked to step outside in other classes, students automatically think that this can't be good for their classmate. In truth, when I got the students outside, I would ask them what's going on. This took away the immediate defensiveness of the students to the talking issue and got them to see that I was interested in them. If they couldn't answer the question, I would prompt them with something like, "All this talking you're doing isn't you. Are you sure that there's nothing wrong?" Students responding to this question will either tell you something or tell you, "nothing." In either case, at this point you will be able to highlight something positive about the students and let them know that other students' as well as their own learning are being affected by their behavior.

If you have been building respect and trust throughout the year, your students should feel grateful that what they got was an interested teacher asking them to change their behavior instead of receiving a punishment. I have had great success with this approach. By eliminating the negative enforcers, I made students feel valued and respected and they appreciated that on some level, and the issue is usually resolved.

Of course, there will always be those students who just don't or won't buy into your "program" and negative enforcers will need to be applied, but that should only be after the class sees that you have given those students every opportunity to correct their behavior by responding to your requests. This will further demonstrate that you care about each of them individually and as a class.

Not Me and Them, but Us Challenge:

Spend five minutes each day just listening and watching your class interact with each other. This can be done just prior to school while waiting for the bell to ring, when they get back from lunch, or packing up to get ready to go home for the day.

When the opportunity presents itself, as it surely will, get involved by asking, "What's going on?" Take it from there and help your students get through their difficulties. Some of you may have counseling services on campus. Feel free to discuss issues with the counselor and refer students to him or her if students and their parents are willing to seek that guidance. Your students will see this as another way you are caring for them and their issues.

Share Goals and Expectations

We all have expectations of one kind or another in life. Most of our expectations are taken for granted. I expect to be able to keep a roof over my head, food on the table, gas in the car, etc. Those are life expectations. As I continued to live my life, I determined what my expectations were, I would create goals then go about doing the things that helped me achieve them.

Our goals are borne out of our expectations. What expectations should I have had as a first-year teacher? Your expectations may have been different from mine, but some of them may have been the same.

My expectations going into my first classroom at a Catholic grammar school, were that my students were there to learn. Because I had been a product of a Catholic education through high school, I also expected that there would be few discipline problems in class.

I had other expectations, but needless to say, it didn't take me long to understand that my expectations were nowhere near the realities of today's students.

What I found was that the majority of students don't really understand why they go to school. They know that they have to, but they look at school as a daily social function with tasks that need to be completed. The concept of learning is something that happens, but not because students are proactive in their own learning.

In fact, it is precisely because students don't know why they are at school that causes discipline problems in the classroom. How many of you have your smartest students cause trouble? How many of you recognize that the students who cause trouble usually don't finish assignments or do homework? Why is that?

I asked myself that very question about three years into my teaching career. It was during the summer before my fourth year as a teacher that I created a lesson plan that would allow me to explore what students thought their responsibility was as a student. I waited until the end of October to engage my students. What I found was surprising.

Almost all of them stated that their responsibility was to get good grades, do all their homework, stay out of trouble, and have fun. What's missing from this list? Only two out of 28 students said that their responsibility was to "learn." I guess you can associate good grades with learning, but why not identify the learning with good grades instead of merely the outcome of hard work? My conclusion was that students fear poor performance more than eagerly embracing the knowledge that is being offered. Even those who get good grades don't learn as much as they could because they don't recognize learning as part of the equation. They see learning as a year full of tasks that need to be completed so that they can get a good grade.

When students are task-oriented without understanding the underlying reason for the task, they may easily check out. Without understanding that the task is meant to impart some knowledge, students may decide to not do the task. I know what you're thinking. Might not students who understand that tasks such as homework, class work, and group discussions are meant to enhance learning also decide to not do the task? They may, but they would be making a choice not to learn as opposed to simply not doing a task.

Once I learned this information, I decided to review my expectations and goals as a teacher. Keep in mind that I had been achieving my goals as I understood them for the first three years, but now it was time to create more challenging goals that hopefully would affect student learning.

What I wanted to accomplish with this class was to have them understand that everything they were asked to do in any class is meant to teach them something. It actually was a hard sell. Students reaching the 7th and 8th grades already "know it all" and don't want to change the way they think about things. As I proceeded to indoctrinate them into a new way of thinking, an amazing thing began to happen. I had fewer and fewer discipline issues and test scores rose. While I couldn't attribute all of this success to their newfound understanding of why they were in school, it's safe to say that it certainly contributed.

How many of you remember asking your own kids what they learned in school today and getting the off-handed "nothing" as a response? When I got that answer from my own two boys before I became a teacher, I would just shake it off as just them not wanting to engage in any school talk. Little did I know that they didn't consider doing class work as learning, but merely tasks that had to be completed. They really didn't think that they learned anything that day.

In an effort to have my students and their parents focus on learning rather than task completion, I created a half-sheet form for students to take home and tell their parents what they learned during the school day. It was the students' responsibility to fill in the form and bring it home. On a regular basis at the end of the school day, I would ask, "What did you learn today?" As they spat out their answers, I wrote them on the board and directed them to select what they had truly learned from the list on the board or one of their own, and fill out the form to take home. I then asked them to bring back the form the next day with a parent's signature on it. Returning the form was a simple way for me to check in on which parents were involved with their students.

As the years went on, I found that most students fell into the same pattern as my fourth class. From that year on, I always introduced the concept of learning as the reason to be in school rather than simply "getting good grades." Many students were able to achieve more than in past years because they understood what was going on in school and why they were there.

Expectation and Goal Challenge:

Here is my challenge to you. Expect that your students are coming to school to learn and not merely to get good grades or because they have to. Teach them this as your expectation and invite them to have it as one of their own.

Set aside a period of time to lead a class discussion on why students come to school. Make it a fun event like a class meeting. Have someone write the answers on the board. Have another student copy the board information onto a notepad. Once your students see what they think the reasons for coming to school are, explore the concept of learning as the prime reason versus simply accomplishing tasks. You and your students should find this discussion both stimulating and enlightening. Type up the responses and pass them out to the class the next day.

Follow up with a lesson on goal setting and ask students to write down three school goals that they want to work on this school year. Let them know that "getting good grades" can't be one of the goals. Have them turn them in, copy them, and let them know that you will be working with them this school year to achieve their goals. From time to time bring out the goals, pass them back to the students, and ask them to attach a short reflection on how they are doing. Write a positive reinforcing comment on each reflection and offer help where you feel it is needed.

I know that it's more work, but the outcome will be worth it for your students, their parents, and you.

The Value of Play Days

I'm sure you've heard the quote, "All work and no play makes Jack a dull boy." Use this concept as part of your strategy to keep students interested in working on good behavior and completed work. It can have an effect on class effort, respect, and morale. Here's how it works.

On the first day of the school year when you hold your class meeting, introduce a concept called "Just 'Cuz Days." You can call it whatever you want. I call it "Just 'Cuz" to make it memorable as a goal on which we as a class will be working. The rules are simple. Students need to do their best without causing behavior issues that take the class away from the lesson of the day. When you feel that this is done consistently, select a day to offer a special treat. This could be things like donuts, Skittles, Starburst, a movie (usually connected to a lesson), or anything else you want to offer as an incentive for your own "Just 'Cuz Day" program. Make it clear that "Just 'Cuz" days will come when unexpected so your students need to stay on task and their best behavior in order to receive a "Just 'Cuz" day.

When you plan a "Just 'Cuz" day, make sure that you know exactly why you are giving students this treat. In the morning, explain that today is a "Just 'Cuz" day and share what you are going to do for them on this day. If it's donuts, you can either give them right at the beginning of the first period or right before recess. If it's something like Skittles or other candy treats, you can give them to them as you are going through a lesson. I use Skittles or Starburst and explain to my students that I am giving them "power pellets" to help them think. I usually let them watch a movie or documentary that is tied to a lesson that I am teaching that week. If they've done especially good work to earn their "Just 'Cuz" day, you may want to include the "power pellets" with the movie.

Another way to reward your class with a "Just 'Cuz" day is to give them some extra recess time out of the blue. Don't announce it in the morning, but find time to go out to recess in the afternoon for 15 minutes or so when there is none scheduled. Once again, make sure to let your students know why they are getting this benefit to their school day.

I usually plan these days for once a month, but don't be afraid to hold them more often if the class is outstanding in its effort to earn one. The more you recognize them for good behavior and effort, the more they will do what is expected.

NEVER take away a "Just Cuz" day from your students for poor behavior. That turns a positive re-enforcer into a negative re-enforcer and will not help you achieve the outcome you seek.

What's the cost of this program you're asking? Well, like any program you implement in your class, it probably won't be part of the school's budget which means that it will all be up to you. Some may be saying, "Why should I be paying students to do what they should be doing on their own?" Don't think of it as pay for performance. Think of it as offering an incentive for good performance. If you find that this program works in your classroom, share it with other teachers and the administration. There may even be an opportunity to add it to the budget. The administration may be able to set aside a specific amount for each teacher in a personal budget that they may use for class activities such as "Just 'Cuz" days.

By offering this type of incentive, your students will be working at doing their best in the classroom by staying focused and self-editing their own behavior. By connecting your "Just 'Cuz" days to a combination of classroom and homework effort, you should have fewer students with missing homework.

Of course, you need to remind your students on a regular basis that the class is working toward its next "Just 'Cuz" day. Ask each student to be responsible in helping classmates achieve the next "Just 'Cuz" day.

The great thing about this type of program is that you don't have to wait until the next semester, trimester, or school year to implement. You can implement it tomorrow. Simply hold a short class meeting, explain the program and let them know that "Today is your first 'Just 'Cuz' day," and give them something to remember why they want to play. Make it something of value so that they want to do what you ask to get to the next "Just 'Cuz" day.

Reinforce the program the next day when they come into the classroom. Don't tell them that you will be doing this once a month. Tell them that it will be totally random based on the behavior and effort you observe in the classroom and in doing homework.

Keep a log of what you see that is good behavior and improvement in homework. Use this log to help you explain why students are getting a "Just 'Cuz" day. Don't use names, just events. You can also use this log to keep track of poor behavior. If you see that it is consistent by an individual student, call them to your desk or outside and let them know that the behavior is unacceptable and it is hurting the class opportunity to earn the next "Just 'Cuz" day. Most students will appreciate the personal contact instead of calling them out in front of the class and will adjust their behavior.

Teacher Homework

This program gives you another tool in your teacher toolbox. Who couldn't use another tool to help with classroom behavior and effort? Try this for six months and evaluate its pros and cons. I think you will be satisfied that you have made a difference in some students' effort and behavior. And, isn't that why we teach, to make a difference in our students' lives?

Be a Coach

What's the difference between a teacher and a coach? Is there a difference? Answer the previous two questions for yourself before you go on.

There truly is a difference, and it's the partnering of the two that can help make you a better teacher. As you teach, you provide your students with the material they need to learn to satisfy the lesson of the day. Some of them get it and some don't. Some will try hard and others won't. How do you teach to both ends of the spectrum? It's difficult to ensure that each student is getting the material you are presenting to them if all you do is teach. Teaching requires you to explain the materials, provide opportunity for practice, and then test for understanding.

By adding coaching to your teaching habits, you can ensure that your students have the best chance for success. Coaching implies a certain effort at trying to make each student better at what they do no matter what subject is being taught. Regardless of class size, coaching can be more rewarding for you as a teacher if applied consistently.

By coaching from day one, your students will see you as something more than just a teacher. That's not to say that there is anything wrong with being seen as a teacher, but, think about it, most students play a sport either at school or out of school. They have been told from a very young age that if they want to get better, they have to listen to what the coach tells them and practice what skills are being taught. How is that different from what you want out of your students in the classroom?

It really isn't. The difference is the level of coaching that goes along with your teaching that can make a difference in your students. Here's where your strategy on homework should be reviewed. There is a certain amount of practice that needs to be done at home, especially in math and in preparation for tests, but I find that most other practice work can be done in the classroom where you can coach.

The best time to coach is when students are doing exercises or answering chapter questions. It's not enough to simply tell your students what to do and then ask them to turn in the paper at the end of the session while you take care of other work that needs to be done such as grading or getting set-up for the next lesson. Coaching requires your full attention in order for it to be meaningful.

Coaching can be done individually or in groups. Either way can be effective so long as you make sure that each student in the group is being coached. How exactly do you coach during practice times? First, make sure that you have covered the lesson completely before giving a practice assignment or exercise. Give complete instructions on what and how you want them to complete the assignment.

Hint: Ask for answers only instead of having students rewrite questions from the book then answering them. This will give you extra time in the classroom to coach to the entire assignment instead of just the questions they had time to complete in class.

Once students have begun the exercise or assignment, walk around to each student or group of students and test with them to see if they truly understand. As a teacher, you obviously know more than they do, so feel free to do more than simply use the book to challenge their thinking. Throw out similar questions that you think will help determine if your student truly understands.

As a coach, you need to inspire desire to do better. You do that by recognizing what a student is doing correctly as well as correcting what is incorrect. Always, always, always begin your coaching session with a positive comment. It can be as simple as "nice handwriting" or "great thinking on that question you answered earlier." Following your positive comment, check-in with the student or students to see how they are doing. Really check the work they are doing to make sure it is the way you want it and that they understand the material. Spend the time you need to ensure that your students understand. Every minute of practice should be spent with you coaching. If you happen to get around the class before your practice period is finished, check in on those students that were struggling earlier. Remember, begin with a positive comment then check the work.

A word about practice – don't rely solely on material in the text for your practice sessions. Create your own practice exercises that parallel what was done in class a day or two earlier. By offering a second practice or "pretest," you will be able to determine who understands the material. It isn't necessary to put all work that is graded into the grade book. Explaining in advance that pretests are for diagnostic purposes only, your students will do their best and be better prepared for the actual test.

Coaching continues even after you have taught the material and done all the practice. It is important to schedule tests as close to teaching the material as you can. It is better to test on small chunks of material such as chapters rather than units - the smaller the better. By breaking material down to its smallest components, you help to ensure that your students won't fail an entire subject because of one bad test. You also have a better vision of what your students are grasping and what they aren't. Never be afraid to re-teach if you find that most students struggled with the test material.

So, the big game (test) is day after tomorrow. How do you prepare your students for taking the test on the material you have just taught and on which you coached them? Do you simply tell them what you will be testing on or do you help them to focus on what's important? Many teachers provide the page numbers that will be tested on and expect students to know all the material. Those teachers who also coach will take the extra step and do a comprehensive review two days prior to a test.

A comprehensive review is a simple way of creating a study guide asking students to take notes as you provide them with information that they should know for the test. You ask questions and have students provide answers. They then write a note that incorporates the question and the answer into a statement of fact. Students now have material to study from for the test. Here is an example, "Who discovered America?" A student answer is, "Christopher Columbus." Students write down the combination of the question and the answer as a piece of factual information, "Christopher Columbus discovered America", and studies that information for the upcoming test. Besides building a body of knowledge that they need to know, you have the opportunity to put other information in the study guide that may not be on the test, but should be known. Consider putting 25-30 questions in the comprehensive review and test on twenty questions. Finally, create 2-3 short essay questions that your students will answer using the material they have studied.

Also, for 10-15 minutes before the test, ask students to test each other using their notes. Drop into each pair or group and play "Stump the Teacher." Have them ask you any question off the list of questions they used to build their study guide for the test. Of course, you need to know the material backwards and forwards to avoid embarrassment.

By coaching as well as teaching, students will have a greater opportunity for success in the classroom. To be a good coach, you have to *always* be coaching. That's not an easy proposition as it requires a lot of "homework" or after school work on your part in grading papers and preparing for the next day's coaching assignments.

Coaching Challenge:

If you have not been coaching in the classroom, ease into it by selecting a subject with which to start. A good choice may be Social Studies or History. There are usually only 5-10 pages in a chapter. Pick out the 25-30 pieces of information you consider important based on the provided test material or based on a test that you create. Do a comprehensive review of the material with your students two days prior to the test and give them 10-15 minutes of study time prior to the test. Watch your students embrace the study process, score better on their tests, and, ultimately, learn the material. ABC - Always Be Coaching!

Positive vs Negative Reinforcement: Acknowledge Good Behavior

While working twenty-one years as a manager for Pacific Bell, I was given some of the most advanced management training in the country. Each year, our skills were updated based on current theories and knowledge. I soaked it up and would be the "go-to" guy for creating local classes for both management and non-management employees.

One of the most unique theories that was presented to us was the concept of "management by walking around." The focus of this style of management is to be visible as a manager, help when you can, and acknowledge the kind of behavior of which you would like to see more. I can hear you now, "That's all well and good, but what does that have to do with teaching?" Really, it has everything to do with both teaching and coaching. Remember, you want to also be perceived as a coach.

In the classroom, there are many opportunities to reward good behavior by a simple comment or some sort of recognition. Long before I became a teacher, when my own children were going to school, I learned that the difference between positive and negative reinforcement is monumental. It's two different ends of a spectrum. There is no middle ground.

My eldest son was in third grade when I had a conversation with his teacher. She would take points away from students for poor behavior. She felt that this was positive reinforcement because each student started with 100 points at the beginning of the semester. I could not get her to see that deducting points was a negative re-enforcer. She asked me what I would do differently. Expecting this question or something like it, I was prepared with an example that I formulated by using my knowledge of management theories. I simply told her to turn it around. Start each student with zero points and make them work for their conduct grade. Create a matrix of what earned points and then reward the good behavior rather than punish the poor behavior. Even after our conversation, she would not acknowledge that she was using negative reinforcement to manage conduct in the classroom.

Needless to say, I remembered that conversation and I used it as a guiding principle when I became a teacher. I didn't know if it would work or not when I was speaking to my son's third grade teacher, so now it was time to find out. In order to measure the differences between the two methods, I used my son's third grade teacher's method of giving each student 100% at the beginning of the report card period telling them what would happen with their grade for specific infractions of the conduct code. While I had many good conduct students during the first semester, there were some that were always losing points and ended up in the "hot seat" during parent/teacher conferences. These were the same students who were in trouble during previous school years and got poor conduct grades. Obviously, because they suffered with poor conduct, the rest of their grades were not as good as they could have been if they had had better conduct in class. As I'm sure you all know, poor conduct diminishes learning.

The next semester, I changed the process and began each student with zero in conduct and gave them a matrix of what would earn them points to achieve the kind of conduct that I wanted in the classroom and they wanted on their report card. Because students had to "choose" to earn their conduct grade, it became an all day opportunity to catch students doing good things; doing right things. It also gave the student who consistently got poor conduct grades and subject grades an opportunity to make a change. Honestly, some did and some did not take advantage of the new process. The encouraging part of this process was that students themselves saw the good behavior being rewarded and worked to emulate it. Conduct grades improved and so did subject grades; not drastically, but there was a positive shift.

"Positive vs. Negative Reinforcement" can be translated into "Reward vs. Punishment." As teachers, what would you really rather do on a consistent basis? Would you rather reward your students or punish them? Granted, there will be times when a student needs an "iron hand" to get the message across, but these students should be fewer because each knows that their conduct grade needs to be earned rather than assumed.

The great part about this process is that you get to acknowledge good behavior and work ethic all day. Not all acknowledgment needs to earn points. Remember, the positive things you do for conduct will carry forward to the desk work you assign and the in-class homework you allow them to do. Simply walk around rather than sitting at your desk grading papers or preparing for the next class. This may be hard to do at times, but the benefits of walking around should make your grading easier. Find students doing well and tell them that you appreciate their effort. Find students that are struggling and help them either in a group or individually. They will appreciate that you care and try that much harder.

There is a positive teacher benefit to finding and acknowledging good behavior and great work ethic. Which do you feel better about at the end of the day, telling students how much you like their effort and work, or how much you need them to change their behavior and improve their effort? I'm guessing that you pretty much would rather go home remembering the good things your students did all day rather than the behavioral things that needed improvement.

This may be an over simplification of the benefit to using positive reinforcement in the classroom along with acknowledging good behavior, but a happy teacher is a better teacher. Use a personal review of the day's successes to prepare for the next day. Energize yourself with the knowledge that tomorrow will reveal even more successes. Live on the positive side of the teacher emotional ledger. Nothing will drag you down faster than expecting a bad day before it even begins.

Effect Positive
Behavior Change

What do you think of when you hear the word "discipline?" I can tell you what your students think of when they hear discipline. They think of punishment.

Which do you use in your classroom? Do you use discipline to correct behavior or to punish it? It's an easy leap from one to the other. What makes one more effective than the other? How do you apply discipline? Is it by sending a disruptive student to after-school detention or do you take the student aside and discuss their behavior one-on-one and request a change in behavior?

I know what you're thinking, "I don't have time to take students aside and work with them one-on-one. They all know the consequences for bad behavior and it's their responsibility to tow the mark." True, but how do your students perceive your sending them to detention? Do they see it as a way to adjust their behavior or do they see it as punishment? I'm pretty sure that if you don't work with your disruptive students one-on-one in some way, sending them to detention will not fix a behavior problem.

Remember that old "respect" mantra that has flowed throughout this book? Well, here it comes again. Respecting students means that you are willing to go the extra mile to get what you need from them. You want them to learn. You can't have disruptive students in class. You have to have enough respect for them to take them aside and explain what their behavior is doing to the rest of the class as well as their own learning. Will they immediately respond? Some will and some may take a few conferences, but by showing them that you respect them enough to have an individual conference with them, you are turning the corner to achieving what you need in your classroom for all to learn.

It was my third or fourth year of teaching when I had to deal with a particularly disruptive class. There wasn't just one student who didn't know why they came to school but at least a half dozen. Students who don't know why they go to school are those who want to do anything but learn. They want to do as little as possible and expect to get by just by virtue of the fact that they are in the class.

Each new school year, I would always assess my students by watching their behavior during the first week or so of classes before I attempted to make any major adjustments. After the first two weeks with this class, it was pretty obvious who the "leader of the pack" was. He was a very bright and intelligent boy, but needed constant approval of his friends. Because of this, a small band of hero-worshipers grew from Kindergarten until they were now in seventh grade. I had been told about them from the sixth grade teacher who had no success whatsoever in correcting their behavior.

I saw this particular class for English, Literature, and Religion. They were not part of my homeroom class. After the first two weeks of school, I gave an in-class reading assignment to the class. While they were reading, I met with them individually to let them know what I observed about their behavior thusfar. I first met with several students whose behavior was average. Then I met with two students whose behavior was exceptional. Finally, I met with the ring leader. In order to be effective in one-on-one discussions, you have to be perfectly honest and not only discuss what behavior you need stopped, but you also need to give your student recommendations on what you would like to see as a replacement behavior. I say recommendations, because the change needs to come from the student, not the teacher. By offering ideas of what could be done differently, the student makes the choice and buys into the concept of changing their behavior because they see it as a good thing.

I spent a little more time with this student than most of the others, but because I respected him enough to involve him in correcting his behavior instead of merely shipping him off to detention, he was able to make adjustments in the way he behaved in class, got better grades, and became a leader in the class. As a leader, he mentored the others who had been his lackeys and assisted me in having them see the error of their ways thus changing their behavior during the course of the year.

Unfortunately, as students respond to respect in a positive way, they also respond to a lack of it by acting out and continuing poor behavior. Since other teachers considered them and treated them as a "band of misfits," it was only a matter of time before most of them were regular attendees at after-school detention.

As the school year progressed, it was obvious that no students from any of my classes were getting detention notices. My peers were perturbed that I was not following the school directives to send students to detention for both minor and major infractions. They just couldn't understand how I claimed to have no behavior issues when they were struggling with this particular class. As we all find out from time to time with things in life, it's hard to change what we do not want to change of our own free will. We find reasons and excuses why this or that won't work instead of investing in a new process and looking for success where there was none before.

Someone once said, "Insanity is doing the same thing over and over again but expecting different results." How many times do you need to send a student to after-school detention before you figure out that their behavior is not changing? What's the next step? Call in the parents? Meet with the principal? Once you've done either of these two options, you have told the student that you are unable to "handle" them and you need assistance. Once you claim to need assistance, you will need it throughout the end of the school year. Don't abdicate your responsibility to find a solution for poor behavior. Work with your student until the behavior is changed.

The concept of one-on-one conferences is not new, but it does end up being rare as a part of a teacher's first line efforts to help students change their behavior. If you have trouble with student behavior in the classroom, consider working with them one-on-one by being honest and open with them. Discuss what the poor behavior is and what options you would like to see as a new behavior. Above all, praise the new behavior as you see it developing. You can do that either in private or as appropriate in front of the class. A mix of both is the most effective.

Finally, in order for this process to work for you, "you have to want to." By deciding that after-school detention is perceived as punishment by your students and won't fix an in-class behavior, you then have to seek another method. Committing to work with students one-on-one in changing behavior will be both rewarding for you and, possibly, life changing for your student. Commit to your student that you can make things better together.

When you boil it right down, we all teach for one reason: To make a difference. Be an agent of change in your students' lives. Respect them. Work with them. Be a part of their success both in the classroom and in life.

Teach Kindness to all Students by your Example

Do you ever find yourself not up to par on some days? We are all susceptible to bad days. The key to bad days is to recognize them and not let your students know that you are having issues outside of school or maybe even within school.

The best way to ensure that you have the right attitude at school is to say "Hi!" to every student you pass on campus. It doesn't matter whether the student is in your class or not. It doesn't matter whether the student is in Junior High or not. Simply say "Hi!" to every student you pass. Make sure and put a smile in your voice and on your face. This action is more for you than for the student, but you both will get something out of it.

For you, this simple action keeps you focused on what you need to be doing for your students, and that is to create a safe and loving environment for them to be in during the time that they are on campus. By personally recognizing each student, you help to create a campus that has fewer barriers between teachers and students. Once again, the fact that you take the time to recognize each student helps to build the trust that is so important in any school's student life.

Has any student ever gotten to you so badly that you felt like throwing a little sarcasm at them? It may make you feel good at the time, and it may put the student in their place, but at what cost?

Sarcasm should be identified as one of the "Deadly Sins" for a teacher. Use of sarcasm has only one purpose and that is to belittle a student. No student is ever made better by a sarcastic teacher trying to correct behavior with this approach. Sarcasm tears at the fabric of trust.

How can a student trust you after you have belittled them in front of the class or in private with a sarcastic remark? We are all human and sometimes it's not easy to control our tongues. We make mistakes and say things that we wish we hadn't. How do you think that we can patch up this tear in trust? It's really quite simple, but it requires that you check your ego at the door. You have to apologize personally to your student and then, if it was in front of the class, apologize to them as well.

By apologizing, you let your students know that mistakes can be fixed. We don't have to live with them. Student lesson learned - the teacher cares enough for us that he or she apologized to us for an unkind remark. If you can, meet with the parent(s) of the student you criticized in public, tell them the circumstances and that you apologized to their child and the class, and let them know you are sorry.

By apologizing to all that may have been harmed by your sarcastic or unkind remark, you take ownership for your actions and show that this is not who you are. If you let it go and think nothing more of it, there's a chance that it could blow out of proportion and cause you disciplinary issues, but the worst part of allowing a poor choice of words to go unfixed is that your students may think less of you because of it.

What happens when you have a tear in fabric? It tends to tear more easily at the weakest point. This is what will happen to the fabric of trust that you are weaving throughout the school year. Don't let it get out of hand. Be big enough to admit your mistake and do the right thing.

The lesson for this chapter is easy enough. Simply say "Hi!" to all students you run into on campus. Use their name if you know it. Say it with a smile in your voice and on your face. If you have time, check in with the student and let them know that you care by taking the time to have a short conversation.

Show your students that you care by living the motto, "Lift each other up, don't tear each other down."

CREATE COOPERATIVE LEARNERS

YOU MAY HAVE HEARD THE TERM "COOPERA-tive learning," but do you really know what that means? Some see it as students working in groups and, to be sure, students cooperating with each other on specific assignments and projects, are part of a cooperative learning process. But cooperative learning can be applied to your teaching style in a way that is as equally beneficial to you. Besides freeing up your time in correcting individual papers, it provides an opportunity for all students to participate in answering questions with immediate feedback thereby effecting learning.

How many of you correct papers by identifying the wrong and right answers? How many of you are current on this exercise? By that I mean, you give students an assignment in class, they turn it in on Monday and you return it to them on Tuesday. Do you take the time to review the exercise answers with them as a class or do you let your "wrong and right" marks do the teaching for you?

I know that there is only a limited amount of time to do all the lessons that you have planned for any given day, so follow-up of yesterday's class and/or homework assignment may not be a priority, but how do you know that all students have learned by your "wrong and right" marks? You can't know. You can only assume that students will review the practice sheets by themselves or with their parents to learn what the sheets and you are trying to teach them.

If you're like me, when you present an English concept or any other subject, you use the text to introduce the current topic. Let's say that you are teaching nouns to your class. You may spend 10-15 minutes going through the examples provided as a learning tool for a specific type of noun. The practice exercises in the text often ask the student to rewrite the sentence identifying the noun based on the lesson. What is the purpose of rewriting the sentence? It takes up time and, while it may improve the students' handwriting, it does little to help them identify nouns or pronouns. I find that class time is better utilized if you simply ask them to write their answers on a sheet of paper. Once the class is finished with the specific exercise(s), go through the exercise in class. Your students get immediate feedback as to whether or not they understand the concept correctly. They get this not only from you, but from other students who help answer the exercise questions orally, cooperatively. They also get the opportunity to ask questions if they don't understand.

Most teachers provide practice sheets either from a workbook or their own handouts. They collect the torn out pages or handouts and then go through them after school at either their desk or at home, returning them to students at their earliest convenience. Their students don't know how well they have done until they get those practice sheets back. We all have lives and families and you know that it is practically impossible to correct every paper each night for return the next day. How do you think a late return may impede the student learning process? Take a minute or two and think about this question.

I know from working with our own two sons who attended Catholic grade school, that, when they received their work back from a teacher, if it didn't have a grade on it, they rarely looked at it to learn from it. As parents, we would review the work and ask questions.

The unfortunate thing in our questioning was that it revealed a negative attitude toward the work borne out of the teacher review process. Some work would be returned a week later. Some work was marked with just the wrong answers asking the students to fix them and return them for another review. My question at this process was, if he didn't get it the first time, how is he going to get it a second time without someone teaching the concept to him? Yes, there is a book and, yes, his parents were available to help him, but wouldn't it have been better to find out at the time the lesson was being taught that he didn't understand the concept?

That is what my concept of cooperative learning is all about; students and teacher working together to learn concepts as a unit instead of as individuals. When answers are shared orally in class, students have the opportunity to ask questions, clarify understanding, and identify areas where they need help. As a teacher using this method, you are able to gauge how well the class understands the concept. By selecting students at random and not just those who raise their hands to answer example questions, you are ensuring that all students stay engaged. They never know when they will be called upon. Each wrong answer is an opportunity to re-teach and/or restate the concept. The more times you validate the concept in open classroom discussion, the greater the opportunity for your students to learn and understand.

This method can be used for any subject that has practice involved. Have students do the work individually then have them provide the answers orally in class. Since you are working as a unit to validate individual work as soon after the lesson is given as you can, homework should be limited. Most work should be done in class with immediate responses to work done on text exercises and/or practice worksheets. By using this method, you free up students' homework time to work on math, writing, reading, and other long-term or short-term assigned team projects.

By using this strategy, both you and your students work together to create a class of cooperative learners; a class of students who find that working through examples together is a part of the learning process and not merely a task that has to be completed with little feedback.

BE CREATIVE: INCLUDE THE
ARTS ANY WAY YOU CAN

UNFORTUNATELY, WHEN MOST SCHOOLS NEED to make budget cuts, there are several "go to" places. It most likely won't be the sports program, and it definitely won't be any of the core curriculum. So, what's left? You know the answer: band, art, glee club, drama, etc. All of these types of classes may be considered as "nice-to-haves" rather than "need-to-haves."

Many studies have been done to justify an Arts curriculum as an integral piece to total learning. But what happens when that piece is cut out? Does that mean it's the end of the Arts connection? It can mean that if you only think of the Arts as a separate class. But what if you think of the Arts in the way that you teach your core subjects? It might be hard to incorporate dance into an everyday lesson, but it wouldn't be so hard to use music as a way to highlight a lesson.

While teaching literature, we would read many short stories that taught life lessons. This one story was about a down-and-out Blues harmonica player who was teaching his new friend the meaning of family. The story finished and the new friend had a new appreciation for his own family and the homeless man went on his way. After reading the story, it was time for another lesson.

Asking for a show of hands, I found out that only five students knew anything about Blues music or how the harmonica was used in that music. I had them put their books away and gave a brief introduction to music in general and Blues in particular. Now, I'm not a music genius. I sing a little, but can't play any instrument at all unless you call the "toilet paper and comb" an instrument. I knew that I wanted to introduce them to this music so I did my homework and bought a few CD's to demonstrate the Blues. After spending some time listening to Billie Holiday and B.B. King, it was time to share what real Blues harmonica sounded like by playing a song from one of the CD's that highlighted the harmonica. Needless to say, the kids got a new appreciation for our story character and for the Blues. Once again, I learned something while teaching my kids.

During a reading of *The Adventures of Tom Sawyer* by Mark Twain, we took a break and I asked my students to take the last chapter that we read, be creative, and draw a scene from the chapter. They needed to use color, do it on a sheet of copy paper, and title it. We took two periods to get them as good as they could be. When we finished, I hung them up around the classroom. My students thoroughly enjoyed the break from their reading, exercised their talent for art, and were ready to continue with our story to see what other adventures Tom and his friends would have. The added benefit was that their work was displayed during the school's open house.

One of the most fun lessons for my students came when I placed students in groups and instructed them to use the characters that we had just read about in a short story, write a script for those characters, and present a short little drama. I let them read their parts as in a readers' theater presentation, but encouraged them to memorize them. I asked them to look around the house and to bring in common items to create costumes and props. It was really fascinating to see the different story extensions that each group of students came up with. So, by doing a little drama such as this, students got to dabble in drama while demonstrating knowledge of the characters that they had just read about.

Finally, listening to classical music or music from musical theatre can be a great resource to drive students' imaginations. Have them listen to a particular piece of music and take notes about what they see in their minds as happening based on the music. Play the piece again so that the students can flesh out the story the music is telling them. Then, have them listen to the music once more to make sure that they have a beginning, middle, and end to the story. Use the next period to have them write a complete story based on the music they heard.

Make sure to use instrumentals; no voices. I have used Beethoven, Mozart, and Leonard Bernstein, to name just a few. The best outcome I ever had was when I played the Prologue to *West Side Story* by Leonard Bernstein. Obviously, students get an opportunity to write and you get an opportunity to read and edit their work. They also get to hear music that they probably wouldn't listen to on their own. Bingo! You've taken care of a writing assignment and introduced classical music to your students all at the same time.

These are only a few ways that you can introduce the Arts into your curriculum. I'm sure that there are many more ideas floating around out there. A good way to tap into ideas for your classroom is to form teacher exchange groups. Meet once at the beginning of the year to share what you expect to do to introduce the Arts into your curriculum, pick up new ideas from your peers, and share your own new ideas during the course of the year via email or further meetings. The best part of working this way is that you can share outcomes. What worked and what didn't. What would you do differently or not at all.

Another way to keep the Arts alive at your school is to encourage the administration to host a school-wide talent show. You can have your student council coordinate it. Ask for specific talents such as singing, dancing, monologues, instruments, etc. You can also sponsor an art show on the same evening as the talent show.

Have you ever heard of "The Gift of Song" presentation to the graduating class? Each class, Kinder through Seventh, either sings a farewell song that already exists, creates a new song by rewriting lyrics to an existing song, or writes a new song altogether. This is best presented in a gym setting where the graduating class can sit in the bleachers and the rest of the school sits on the gym floor waiting for their turn to perform. Each class from Kinder to Seventh performs their special song of farewell. Students can dress in costume and/or use instruments such as maracas or tambourines or CD's or nothing at all to present their song. I always used the rewrite-a-song method for my seventh graders. The last song we did for our graduating eighth graders was a rewritten version of *Don't Stop Believing* by Journey.

One final tip for keeping the Arts alive in your classroom and maybe even in the whole school is to look for community theatre presentations that support your curriculum, and plan a field trip. Follow-up on the field trip with in-class discussions and writing assignments as you see fit.

While the Arts may go away as a formal part of the curriculum, they don't have to disappear altogether. Be creative. Keep the Arts alive in your school simply by applying them to your curriculum. Believe me, your students will enjoy their lessons more and you will enjoy teaching more when you expand beyond simple "book learnin'."

The nice thing about applying the Arts to your curriculum is that you don't have to wait for them to go away before you add them. All of the techniques identified above can be used in your existing coursework. To coin a phrase from Mikey of Life cereal fame, "Try it! You'll Like It!"

BE FLEXIBLE: DO WHAT OTHERS ARE AFRAID TO DO

As you all know, there's more to teaching than just being in the classroom with your kids. Someone has to run the student council, spelling bee, academic decathlon, geography bee, speech contest, year book, and many other activities that give your school its distinct personality and offers opportunity for students to learn and be of service.

Don't shy away from these extra duties. Find the ones that you are good at and volunteer to mentor or lead them. In addition to helping your school, you should feel a sense of satisfaction knowing that your students are getting to work with *you*, the best that your school has to offer in your selected extracurricular endeavor.

So, why else should you volunteer for assignments that it seems no one else wants? The obvious answer is that it provides you an opportunity to distinguish yourself among your peers. Secondarily, you may learn something along the way. For a teacher, teaching is all about learning – not only student learning but also teacher learning. You should be learning something new from your kids each day. Here is an opportunity to add to your knowledge.

I can hear you now, "I'm the teacher, what can they teach me?" It's a good question, but the truth is that, while your students may not personally teach you something new every day, you still have the opportunity to learn as you prepare for the day's lessons. Hopefully, not many of you ever go into a new day just relying on the books in front of you. There is always something extra that can be added to your lectures by "scavenging" the internet to add to your body of knowledge and, ultimately, to your students' body of knowledge.

Some of the information you bring to the classroom is for background purposes and you share it as such. You may want to include some of that information on the next test. Let them know up front that you will be including this information on the test. Make sure that they are taking notes so that they can be successful when testing.

You may already have your students taking notes as you lecture and interact with them in discussion from the text. That's a good practice for when they get to high school and college. By giving them a hint of what will be on the test, you are ensuring that they study exactly what they need to know. Of course, you don't tell them everything that will be on the test, but you do give them enough information so that they spend time studying meaningful information from the unit. Nothing is worse for a student than when they spend several hours studying for a test only to learn that they spent time studying things that were insignificant to the information you needed them to know. With all of the homework and extracurricular activities that students have, providing them with information to focus on when studying for a test provides them a map to the finish line. Your efforts will be appreciated and increase the respect and trust that you seek with your students.

So, how does flexibility enter into this conversation? The key here is to understand who you are thinking of when you hear the word "flexible." Do you mean your students, other teachers, the administration, parents, or yourself? Actually, being flexible with all of these constituents will provide you an opportunity to show that you truly care about your students and not merely the process of educating them.

While in the classroom, I was always seen as someone who could be trusted to make changes to accommodate others. Sometimes this meant changing a test date because there were too many tests scheduled by other teachers on the same date. Sometimes this meant taking extra students in my class while another teacher took care of an issue. Sometimes it meant taking on tasks that meant extra time after or before school. Why would I want to do that? In most cases, there really is only one reason; it's the right thing to do.

If you consistently strive to do the right thing in all circumstances, the decision to be flexible is an easy one. I once worked with a teacher who gave an assignment that none of her AP students picked up on. The due date came and not one student turned in the assignment. The teacher stuck with her due date and deducted a grade for each student that did not meet the due date. What would you have done in a case like that? Would you make an allowance or just assume that all the students got together and decided not to turn the assignment in on time?

Are we perfect as teachers? Do we control our classrooms by being dictators? What is our goal as teachers? First, perfect we're not. We make mistakes. How we respond to those mistakes demonstrates our character to our students. That is a life lesson. By doing the right thing in all circumstances, we build respect with our students. Students should not have to feel afraid of punishment simply for being kids.

We as teachers can find ways to take what students perceive as harmless play in the classroom and turn it into a positive learning experience. For instance, ask students who are a little out of line if they know the lesson. Some will challenge you, but most will say "no." Most often, those who say "no" will be back in line. Invite those who challenge you and say "yes" up to the podium to continue teaching the lesson. They may take you up on it. Don't be afraid to let them try. In fact, as they teach the lesson, don't be afraid to guide them by asking questions and expecting answers. At some point in their presentation, they will be at the end of what they think they know. Thank them for helping and continue with the lesson, validating what the student taught or correcting any irregularities.

The goal of each of us as educators is to teach. Pretty much a given, but how and what we teach can be somewhat open to interpretation. Sure, we teach to State curriculum standards, but we teach so much more than that. What did I teach my students by letting them teach my class for five minutes? I taught them that I valued them even when they were not 100% engaged in the process. I taught them that I trusted them enough to turn the class over to them. I taught them that being a part of the class was important and that the class learns when they learn. Now, what did the class learn by my inviting students to teach them? The response by my students was to become completely engaged with what was being taught by their peer. They learned the lesson and were supportive of their classmate. Besides the lesson, they learned something about team building.

I suppose I could have simply threatened my disruptive student with after school detention and used that negative reinforcement, but I always look for a way to turn any situation into a teaching opportunity. I guess you could say that my mantra is, "Always be Teaching."

Being flexible should be an integral part of your teaching style. Don't feel as though you lose control because you are being flexible. The fact is that you are more in control when you can be flexible with students, teachers, administration, and parents.

I learned this truth in my second year as a teacher. It was during parent/teacher conferences and I had an irate mother meet with me demanding to know how I could have given her daughter a "C" in English when she had never had any grade below an "A" in all her time at the school. This grade would keep her off the honor roll for the semester. I showed the mom my grade book indicating that there were several missing assignments. I had given her daughter several opportunities to turn in the work, but she didn't. I did what any of you would do. I gave her the grade she deserved.

I knew going into this conference that her parents would need to be convinced of the grade so I came prepared. I believe that most of you would have explained the situation and left the grade as is and taught the student and parents a lesson in responsibility that would have had the negative consequences of keeping the student off of the honor roll. My approach was a little different.

My goal in the classroom is always to make sure that students get knowledge by doing the work that I assign. I could have asked the parents to have their daughter finish the assignments and make no change to the grade or have her do the work and change the grade to reflect that it was late instead of missing. She did the work and it was "A" quality as I knew it would be. I gave her a "B" for the late assignments which brought her course grade up to a "B+" and allowed her to be put on the honor roll.

By being flexible, I was able to teach responsibility as well as have my student get the knowledge I wanted her to have. The mom was happy, my student saw me as an ally in her education, and I never had a late assignment from her again in the next two years of her attending my classes.

Finally, find a school assignment that you can be the best at, accept it willingly, and look for ways to be flexible within your school community. You will be seen as a teacher who is indeed looking out for the best interests of your students and the school.

CHECK IN WITH STUDENTS ON A REGULAR BASIS

EACH OF US IN THE TEACHING PROFESSION has gone through an education process that is designed to make us the best teachers that we can be. How do we know whether or not we have achieved being the best teacher that we can be? Peers support us during the school year, principals and others sit in on class sessions and provide oral feedback. You may even receive a written review of what you did well and what needs improvement.

All these interactions are meant to improve us as teachers, and they are very important. In my teaching career, I found that there was one other constituency that was just as important - my students.

What's the best way to know if you are getting through to students? Sure, their grades will tell you that they know how to study or not, but what tells you that you are doing a good job in teaching them on a daily basis? During my time teaching, I established a process that would keep me grounded in knowing what worked and what didn't.

Near the end of the first trimester, I would take one period and turn it into a free reading period as I'd call up each student and ask them just three questions: 1) Are you having any issues with anyone in the class? 2) What am I doing that helps you learn? 3) What can I do better to help you learn?

I know what you're thinking. What am I going to do with this information? The answer to that question depends on what answers you get from your students. The answer to the first one will most likely be "no", but it lets your students know right off the bat that you care about them in the context of class dynamics. If they say "yes", gather what information you can and determine if you need to get involved or simply offer suggestions on how they can reconcile with the other student or students. Let your student know that you want them to let you know if they can't reconcile the issue.

The second question will require your students to take a little time to think about you and your skills. Don't let them get off by saying something like, "I can't think of anything." Let them know that you would like at least one thing that you are doing that is helping them during the school year. If they can't think of anything at your visit, ask them to think about it and write up a short answer and turn it in the next day. This usually will make them think of something so that they don't have to write anything at night.

Question three is where the meat of this little exercise exists. Wouldn't you like to know what students need from you with regards to how you teach them? Some students may not need anything more than what you are giving them, but others may need help with what you do on a daily basis.

One year I had a student who couldn't read cursive and I didn't find out about it until almost three weeks into the trimester when he turned in his notebook for review and there was nothing but rubbish. When I questioned him as to why he hadn't been keeping good notes, he told me that he couldn't read my cursive on the board and tried to take notes as I was speaking. Could I fix his inability to read cursive? No, but I could change the way I put notes on the board. So, for the rest of the year, I printed my notes on the board. I found it more difficult, but my student had a complete notebook each time I reviewed it. This is just another example of being flexible to achieve success.

Make sure that your students know that you are serious about question three and that you want them to be honest so that you can help them be as successful as they can be during the school year.

During the second trimester while doing seat work, you may want to call up several students whom you know are doing well and simply thank them for doing their best. Call up all those whom you perceive are not doing well and find out what you can do to implement a change in their ability to be successful with their work.

One year I had a student who had low grades because he did not know how to write complete sentences. I began working with him in the classroom and he got a little better, but not enough to raise his grades. When he told his mother that I was helping him, she came to see me to thank me. I knew that there was not enough time in the day to properly tutor her son, so I asked if she would be interested in having him stay after school on Wednesdays to practice thinking about writing and writing what he was thinking about. She and he both said yes and I tutored him for five months. His writing ability improved and so did his grades. No,

I did not get paid for tutoring him to write. I considered it just part of what it means to be a teacher and a coach.

The final way I used to discover how well I did in the classroom was to create a Teacher Report Card. During the last week of school, I handed out the Teacher Report Card geared to have students tell me what worked and what didn't work for them during the school year. The report card had specific questions that were open-ended and needed explanation rather than a simple "yes" or "no" answer.

Because I had been checking in throughout the year, most of the answers were what I expected, but one year I got a battery of answers from one girl that I didn't expect. Her responses made me think about how I could have missed her displeasure with my teaching methods. After reading her responses over and over, I started to see how I could do things a little differently the next year that may make a difference for the whole class. On the last day of school, I had a short conversation with her apologizing for not doing my best for her, but also thanking her for giving me a roadmap for the next school year. She thanked me and left saying, "Have a great summer. I look forward to being in your class next year." I guess it wasn't that bad of a year for her after all.

Bottom line is that, if you never ask, you'll never know how well you are doing. Accept the criticism and learn from it. You will be a better teacher for it.

Finally, Never Give Up

So you've read through this book several times and you've tried some of the skills mentioned. Some of them worked well and others were less successful. As with anything new, getting it right the first time every time is next to impossible. The old adage, "practice makes perfect", needs to be applied to these strategies and techniques.

Each time you implement a new technique, whether or not it was successful, you should analyze what went right and what didn't go so right. By analyzing both successes and failures, you will be able to determine how to tweak the specific technique to fit your individual students, the entire class, and your own strategies.

"Never give up" is a term you hear from many self-help gurus who use it as a mantra to instill confidence in their clients. It might sound trite, but it truly is the golden rule for practically all successful people. Where would we be if, after failing in his early designs, Thomas Edison had given up on development of the electric light? You can say that about almost anyone who has desired to implement a new idea, product, or service.

Never giving up requires belief and commitment - belief in what you are trying to implement, and commitment to seeing it through to the end. It's not as easy as it sounds. How do you turn belief and commitment into success?

First, believing in the process has to be more than just spoken. It has to be borne out of understanding how the principles interact and what to expect as an outcome of implementation. You have to have a desire to make a change and commit to see it through to the end. Any time there is change in your life, you have to first accept it then embrace it.

When I worked at Pacific Bell (now AT&T), products and processes were constantly changing. While many of my peers chose to fight the changes, those of us who understood why they were necessary and, not only accepted them, but embraced them, were able to lead our teams to be successful with the new changes. Once you believe in the process, it then becomes a matter of committing to doing all you can to implement the change with your own teaching style and strategies.

Each new school year, you have an opportunity to begin with a clean slate; an opportunity to implement any new changes you wish to make and reinforce those you have already made. It's not enough to go into the classroom each year with the same process as you've used since forever. Why not, you ask? The main reason is that you run the risk of becoming stale in the classroom.

Being stale may lead to a lack of enthusiasm, loss of interest in your subject, and, potentially, loss of interest in your students. The last thing you want is to come to school each day dreading the process because it has become boring. Keep it fresh by implementing regular change in both the way you teach the curriculum, and the way you work with students.

Never give up! Do it again and again and again until you have perfected it. Do it again and again, but better next year.

Good luck and I'll leave you with a phrase I used with all my students that put the responsibility on them to effect their academic and behavioral changes: "You just gotta wanna!" You just have to want to do it better next time! It's all up to you!

To book speaking engagements for your teachers, contact Don Marsolais at the following email address. Please provide your name, position, school name, city, and contact number.

dpmarsolais@surewest.net

CPSIA information can be obtained
at www.ICGtesting.com
Printed in the USA
FSHW020909180321

9 781662 801228